S0-ABT-543

# Body in the Group

## OCEAN ADVENTURE

Social Thinking Publishing, San Jose, California
www.socialthinking.com

**Body in the Group**
Ocean Adventure

Ryan Hendrix, Kari Zweber Palmer, Nancy Tarshis and Michelle Garcia Winner

Copyright ©2013 Think Social Publishing, Inc.
All rights reserved. This book may not be copied in its entirety for any reason.
Pages may be copied for in-classroom or in-clinic use with students or for educating
other professionals in a free in-service training. All other reprinting prohibited without
written permission of publisher.

The following terms are registered trademarks belonging to Social Thinking Publishing:
Social Thinking®
Superflex®

Visit www.socialthinking.com for additional information on our trademarked and copyrighted terms, their
use by others, including citation and proper attribution.

ISBN: 978-1-936943-10-4

Social Thinking Publishing
3031 Tisch Way, Suite 800
San Jose, CA 95128
Phone: (877) 464-9278
Fax: (408) 557-8594

This book is printed and bound in Tennessee by Mighty Color Printing.
Books may be ordered online at www.socialthinking.com.

# Introduction

*The Incredible Flexible You*™ is an engaging new Social Thinking educational series targeted to children ages 4-7. It combines a social learning framework used in schools, homes and clinical settings around the world with music and dramatic play activities that will appeal to early learners.

The series introduces Michelle Garcia Winner's Social Thinking Vocabulary© and concepts to children in preschool and the early elementary years. It consists of 10 storybooks plus related curriculum, released in two volumes. TIFY, as we lovingly call it, is designed to help our young ones create the mental and emotional connections needed for social communication and social awareness.

Appropriate for all kids, the TIFY curriculum was specially designed to help promote social learning in children with Asperger Syndrome, high functioning autism spectrum disorders, hyperlexia, ADHD, social behavior problems, or those with social communication disorders.

## Storybook 4

While we often realize the importance of verbal language and what to say in a conversation, it is important to understand that physical proximity is also a key ingredient to successful social interactions. In storybook 4, we teach that keeping your *body in the group* means maintaining a comfortable physical presence around others – not too close, yet not too far away. When your body is in the group, it sends the nonverbal message that you are interested in others and that you are following the same plan. The opposite is also true. If your body is out of the group – it is too far away – it sends the message you are not thinking about the group.

### The Curriculum & Lessons

Play is the avenue through which our young children learn and practice their social thinking and social skills, and our curriculum is built on the idea that learning should be fun and playful! Each storybook is aligned with a lesson plan and authors walk educators or parents through the lessons from start to finish. Teaching moment icons call attention to those places to Stop and Notice, Stop and Discuss, or Stop and Do so adults capture the opportunities to take teaching and learning to a deeper level. Within each individual lesson, teachers find hands-on activities, structured play, dramatic activities and lively songs to motivate kids to learn.

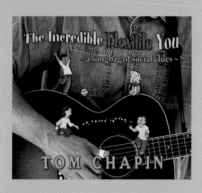

## Tom Chapin and Phil Galdston talk about creating magic in the music and songs of TIFY.

*In The Group* began with the chant, "Everybody has a body, keep your body in the group," which we liked because it's inclusive, nails the message, and the three "body's" link together to make a very catchy phrase.

For the verses, Tom invented a little number game, "If it's one, make it two. Make it me and you. If it's two, make it three, you and you and me...", etc. This is not only fun, it helps illustrate the concept and leads directly into the chorus.

The key to recording the song was Phil discovering a wonderfully funky New Orleans drum pattern, which suggested the wah-wah guitar, to which we added a couple of key changes, and, finally, a gospel choir featuring the saucy Lucy Woodward.

Learn more at tomchapin.com and theincredibleflexibleyou.com.

## The Magic that Music Brings to Learning

The TIFY series is accompanied by *The Incredible Flexible You* music CD with songs created by longtime songwriters and Grammy-recognized artists Tom Chapin and Phil Galdston. To illustrate the powerful ideas underlying Social Thinking, these talented artists went back to the core reason artists combine words and music: to *communicate*. Tom Chapin, widely known for empowering children through his music, co-wrote and performs 12 engaging songs that reinforce the Social Thinking concepts. His fresh, catchy, singable songs appeal to parents, teachers and especially young children, get them up and moving, and enhance their ability to synthesize Social Thinking Vocabulary into everyday life. (Read more at left about their inspiration for the music for this storybook.)

When used in combination, the storybooks, curriculum and music CD create a powerful teaching tool that inspires teachers and students, or parents and kids, to experience together what social thinking is all about.

*The Incredible Flexible You* series is available at socialthinking.com.

4

Evan, Ellie, Jesse and Molly are swimming in the ocean.

There is so much to see and do! They notice a lot of sea creatures.

Some are in groups and some are not.

Look at the fish. We know they are a group
because their bodies are together. They are not too close or too far.
They are swimming and moving in the same direction.
And over there is a group of jellyfish.
Their bodies are together. They are in a group.

Stop and Notice

Stop and Do

Evan, Ellie, Jesse and Molly have their bodies in a group too.

They are not too close and not too far.

Jesse has an idea – they can look for a shark tooth together!

The kids agree and the group plan is to find a shark tooth.

Nobody knows where to find one so they will have to work together.

The kids decide to swim to the coral reef.

Maybe they will find a shark tooth there.

Oops! Their bodies got too close to each other.

Stop and Notice

Now everyone has their bodies in the group again
and they are not too close.

Stop and Notice

Now their bodies are too far away from each other!
Oops! They are not a group.

Stop and Notice

The kids put their bodies together in a group and swim over the coral. The
plan is to find a shark tooth. They think with their eyes and look all around.
They see a group of fish playing school.
No shark tooth here! They'll have to keep looking.

12

Next, the group swims through a seaweed jungle. Maybe the shark tooth is hiding here! Oops! Evan's body is out of the group. The other kids think he doesn't want to look in the seaweed with them.

That makes them feel confused.

Evan puts his body back in the group. Now Ellie, Jesse and Molly know he wants to look for the shark tooth with them. That makes them all feel good.

The kids think with their eyes and search all around.

They see crabs but no shark tooth!

Stop and Notice

Up ahead they see a sunken ship. Maybe they can find a shark tooth there!
Evan, Ellie and Jesse swim toward the ship. Oops!
Molly's body is out of the group. The other kids think she doesn't want to
look in the ship with them. They feel sad.

Molly puts her body in the group. Now Evan, Ellie and Jesse know she wants
to look for the shark tooth with them. They all feel happy.
The kids think with their eyes and search all around.
They see a group of sea turtles but no shark tooth!

Stop and Notice

In the distance, the kids see a dark sea cave. There HAS to be a shark tooth somewhere in there. Oops! Ellie's body leaves the group. The other kids think she doesn't want to find the shark tooth with them. They feel upset.

Ellie puts her body back in the group.
Now Evan, Jesse and Molly know she wants to go inside
the sea cave with them. They all feel excited.

The kids put their bodies in the group and search inside the sea cave.

They have to turn on their flashlights because it is so dark!

Evan thinks with his eyes and sees something...

Hmmm... what is that?

Ellie joins Evan and they become a group.

She looks and sees a shiny eye.

Hmmm... what could that be?

Molly puts her body in their group.

She sees a fin.

Hmmm....

Jesse puts his body in the group and sees a shark tooth.

Finally, they found a shark tooth!

But wait — it's not JUST a shark tooth...

Stop and Discuss

It's a SHARK!

Evan, Ellie, Jesse and Molly put their bodies in the group
and swim, swim, swim away as fast as they can!

Bodies in the group. Through the sunken ship! Swim, swim, swim!

Bodies in the group. Through the seaweed! Swim, swim, swim!

Bodies in the group. Through the coral! Swim, swim, swim!

Bodies in the group. Swim, swim, swim!

Look — it's the boat up ahead!

Bodies in the group. Back on the boat!
Phew! Time to go home.